San Antonio: The River City

Margarita González-Jensen

Contents

Rigby®
A Harcourt Achieve Imprint

www.Rigby.com
1-800-531-5015

Introduction:
Places Change and Grow

Have you ever thought about what your town or city looked like hundreds of years ago? Some places begin as small towns and stay small. Other places grow into large cities and change over time.

San Antonio has grown from a small village to a large city.

San Antonio is an old city in Texas that began as a small village on a river. Settlers from Spain first began to build the city of San Antonio 50 years before the United States became a country! Today San Antonio is the ninth largest city in the United States. Different events and interesting people have helped San Antonio grow and change over the years.

3

Chapter 1
Life Along the River

Many years ago, Native American groups lived in central Texas. These Native Americans needed animals to hunt, fish to catch, and fruit and nuts to gather. Because the wooded area along a beautiful river provided all of this, these Native Americans settled there. They named the river *Yanaguana,* which means "clear waters."

Rivers gave Native Americans and settlers water that they needed to live.

In 1691 Spanish explorers traveled through this area and renamed the river the San Antonio River. Almost 30 years later, soldiers, other Spanish explorers, and religious people settled along the San Antonio River. These new settlers, with the help of the Native Americans, began building a **mission,** a small religious building. They called this mission *San Antonio de Valero.* It later became known as the Alamo.

San Antonio

San Antonio River

5

Life in the Missions

Soon the settlers built four more missions along the river. Originally, people used them as religious centers, schools, government offices, hospitals, and homes for some Native Americans and religious leaders. The missions had high, thick walls, which helped protect the people inside from attacks. The church was the most important building in the mission, while the buildings around it were for living, working, learning, and cooking.

Fun Fact

The San Antonio Missions became a national historical park in 1978.

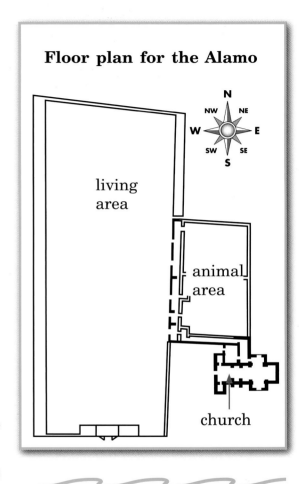

Floor plan for the Alamo

living area

animal area

church

This is how one mission, the Alamo, was laid out.

The San Antonio River was important to the people living in San Antonio.

This area around the missions and the river became known as *La Villita,* or small village, and was named San Antonio. When people moved to San Antonio, they often lived and worked near the river. Even the King of Spain sent families to live in San Antonio. People would use the water from the river for drinking and watering crops. People also went to the river to relax. The river helped all of the people new to the area build a community. Years later this land around the San Antonio River would attract **immigrants** from Europe who settled in Texas.

Chapter 2
San Antonio Grows

By the early 1800s, San Antonio was becoming the largest town in Texas, which at that time was part of Mexico. Over 2,000 people called San Antonio their home!

Soon many Mexicans living in Texas, new immigrants, and **frontierspeople** wanted Texas to be independent from Mexico. These people formed an army and began fighting for Texas independence in 1835.

Some of the missions were burned as people fought to free Texas from Mexico's rule.

After the war was over, Texas became independent from Mexico. In 1842 Mexicans seized San Antonio twice, so the population went down to 800 as people died or left for safety.

After Texas became part of the United States, people came back to San Antonio. The town had a good location in the center of Texas, so it attracted people who wanted to move west from the East. By 1860 San Antonio was again the largest town in Texas.

| Population in San Antonio ||
Year	Population
1776	2,060
1845	800
1850	3,488
1860	8,235
1880	20,550

Cowboys and Cattle Drives

Cowboys also helped San Antonio grow. Texas had millions of longhorn cattle that provided food for people in the East. By 1860 cowboys began moving cattle through San Antonio on their way to other states. These were called **cattle drives.**

Mexican cowboys, called *vaqueros,* were very skilled with ropes called lassos. Lassos were important on cattle drives for keeping the cattle together. Ranchers from south Texas and even Mexico drove their cattle to San Antonio stockyards. (Stockyards were places to keep cattle before moving them somewhere else.)

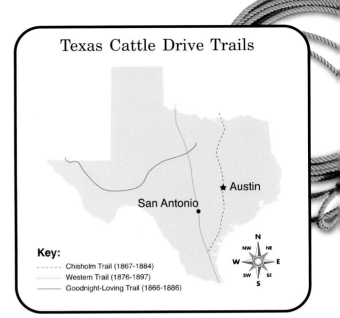

Texas Cattle Drive Trails

Austin

San Antonio

Key:
Chisholm Trail (1867-1884)
Western Trail (1876-1897)
Goodnight-Loving Trail (1866-1886)

N
NW NE
W E
SW SE
S

Once the cattle arrived in states like Kansas, Montana, and New York, they were sold for a lot of money. People who lived in these states and many other states wanted Texas cattle because they seldom got beef where they lived.

Fun Facts

- Some cowboys on cattle drives were as young as 12 years old!
- Longhorn cattle could live by eating weeds and cactus and drinking very little water on a cattle drive.
- A longhorn weighs as much as a small car.

11

Railroads

San Antonio got its first railroad in 1877. Then people had a new way to move cattle to other states more quickly. The trains also brought more business and more people to San Antonio. The city saw its population rise to almost three times more than it was after the war with Mexico.

This is a train station in San Antonio in the early 1900s.

More than twenty years later, there were five railroads serving the city, and San Antonio was growing larger and larger. People from all over had to travel through San Antonio to get to other places. Even today one of the main railroad lines across Texas still runs through San Antonio.

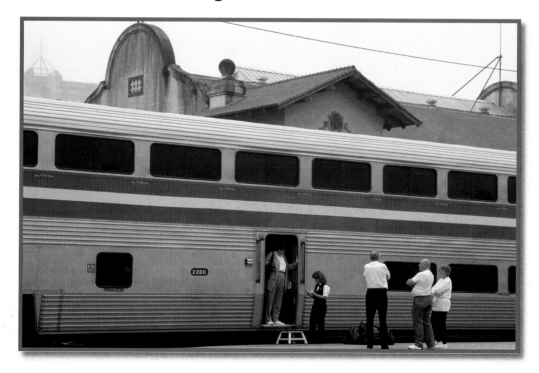

This is a modern train in San Antonio.

Traveling in San Antonio Today

Today San Antonio still has its railroads, but there are also other ways for people to get from place to place in the city. People built bridges to connect one side of the San Antonio River with the other. One famous bridge is the Commerce Street Bridge, which was built in 1915. It has an image of a Native American carved into it as a reminder of the first people who lived in San Antonio.

Today the San Antonio River has many bridges crossing over it.

This is one of the many bridges that crosses over the San Antonio River.

People also use freeways to get around the city. After the car was invented in the early 1900s, many people bought cars so they could drive around San Antonio. In the 1940s, builders created roads to link different parts of the city so people could move quickly from one place to another. Today millions of vehicles travel on the many San Antonio freeways every day!

Chapter 3
Spending Time in San Antonio

Visiting the River City

Visitors come to San Antonio from all over the world. When people come to the city, they are reminded of how the city began long ago. When walking along the San Antonio River, people can see shops and restaurants that were originally built by the Spanish settlers and the immigrants from Europe.

This is the entrance to *La Villita*.

Visiting Museums

People also like to spend time in San Antonio because it honors the people and different ways of life, or **cultures,** that have made it a great city.

For example, the Guadalupe Cultural Art Center is a museum that shows the arts and preserves the culture of Chicano, Latino, and Native American people who have lived in San Antonio for hundreds of years. People at the museum have music, such as *conjunto* music, dance, art, and theater events all year long and invite the community to join them in keeping these cultures alive in the city.

A *conjunto* band includes guitar players, an accordion player, and a drummer.

Visiting the Missions

Visitors to San Antonio also like to see the Spanish missions, which remind people of the city's history. The insides of the missions still have examples of Native American and Spanish art. Many people like to visit the Alamo, the mission where many people died during the war for independence with Mexico. Today the mission has a museum that includes tools and crafts from hundreds of years of Texas history.

inside the Alamo

view of one of the missions

paintings at one of the missions

Visiting the Train Stations

Because the railroad was important in San Antonio's history, people enjoy visiting the train stations that still exist in the city. One station is called the Sunset station, and when it was built in 1903, people could ride trains through this station on a trip across the country. Another railroad station built by the International & Great Northern Railroad was built in the same style as the Spanish missions. This train station looks as if it is the outside of the Alamo!

This is the Sunset Train Station.

San Antonio Photo Essay

Because the San Antonio River has been such a big part of San Antonio's history, people wanted to make the area around it a place where visitors could enjoy the sights and learn about the city's past. One of the most beautiful sights on the river is the River Walk, which is in the center of the city. The following photo essay shows pictures of the River Walk today.

The Tower of the Americas This restaurant allows people to eat and enjoy the view of San Antonio at the same time.

The Cos House

This building, which is one of the oldest buildings in *La Villita,* is often used for weddings and dinners today.

Arneson River Theater

This outside theater has grass seats on one side of the river and a patio-type stage on the other where shows take place.

River Center Mall
This mall has over 125 stores and restaurants.

Republic of Texas Restaurant
This restaurant is known for its Tex-Mex food, which combines the best tastes from both Texan and Mexican cooking.

From looking at the photo essay, you can see that there are many places to visit along the River Walk in San Antonio. Which place would you visit first?

Casa Río Restaurant
Boats pass by this Mexican restaurant, which makes its own thick corn tortillas.

Glossary

cattle drives moving cows from one place to another

cultures the art, beliefs, and customs of a group of people

frontiers people people who lived on the edge of a settled town or land

immigrants people who come to one country from another country

mission a small religious building

Index